Dry fly

Muddler fly

Mini-lure

Fly imitation

Streamer fly

Swimfeeder

DK SUPERGUIDES
ANGLING
JOHN BAILEY

Playing a fish

Bluegill

Soft frog lure

Starting out

Thunderbug spinner

Shallow diver

A DORLING KINDERSLEY BOOK

Dorling  Kindersley

LONDON, NEW YORK, SYDNEY, DELHI, PARIS,
MUNICH and JOHANNESBURG

Senior Editor Fiona Robertson
Senior Art Editor Rebecca Johns
Managing Editor Mary Ling
Managing Art Editor Rachael Foster
Photography Steve Gorton
DTP Designer Almudena Díaz
Production Kate Oliver
Picture Research Jamie Robinson

The young anglers
Carlene Davis, Harry Devenish, Joanne Gittins, Kristofer Learoyd

80 Strand, London WC2R 0RL
First published as *The Young Angler*, 1999
This edition printed in 2006

2 4 6 8 10 9 7 5 3

A CIP catalogue for this book is available from the British Library.

ISBN 0 7513 1362 9

Colour reproduction by Colourscan, Singapore
Printed and bound in China by L.Rex

see our complete
catalogue at
www.dk.com

Contents

"The taimen is one of the rarest freshwater fish in the world."

To all young anglers

"**C**ONGRATULATIONS! YOU HAVE DECIDED to take up fishing, in my mind absolutely the best sport in the world. You will find that it takes you to fascinating waters of great beauty, that you catch spectacular fish, learn new skills, and make new friends. Above all, you will experience wild excitement. Perhaps it will be when the first float goes under, or when a trout rises to take in your fly. Then the reel will shriek, the rod will buckle in your hands, your heart will beat like a drum and you will know exactly why you've become an angler. Best of luck and tight lines every day you fish. **"**

"This fish was caught in a very remote river in Mongolia. It took me several trips to track the species down."

John Bailey

"This golden mahseer has big scales and huge fins."

"Here I am returning a really super pike to the waters of the Baltic Sea. Big fish in clear water offer great excitement!"

"Mahseer are the hardest fighting freshwater fish in the world. They inhabit the quick, clean rivers of India and attract anglers from all over the globe."

"I am kneeling to land a beaut[i]ful Arctic char that has just come u[p] from the sea into one of the rive[rs] in Greenland. Even though I a[m] north of the Arctic Circle, it is still warm enough to do a bit of sunbathing."

"One of my favourite rods – one that I have had for 20 years!"

"Although I love to travel to differ[ent] countries, I still have time for the ponds and pools where I learned [my] fishing back in my childhood. Here I am hoping for a carp or a pike.

4

History of angling

FOR AS LONG as people have been on Earth, they have wanted to go fishing. In very early times, fishing was just another way of catching food. However, for at least 3,000 years, fishing has also been a sport. The Egyptians and the Romans fished for fun, as have countless men, women, and children ever since. Tackle has improved enormously since those early days and with the development of space-age materials, it looks likely to continue changing.

Roman pursuits

This engraving dates from the 3rd century BC and supports the theory that the Romans were keen fishermen. For the more wealthy Romans, fishing was most definitely a sport, and one that they could enjoy in all the far-flung corners of their empire. Rods were made of either wood or bone, but the hooks were not dissimilar to those used today.

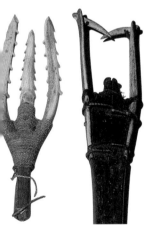

Spears

Spears have been used to catch fish for many hundreds of years and are in fact still used, particularly in the waters of the South Seas. There is a real art to this way of fishing, as you have to take refraction into account. This is the way that the surface reflection distorts the position in which the fish is lying.

Words of wisdom

The Compleat Angler, published in 1653, is one of the most famous fishing books ever written. It has been published in more than 300 editions and still contains sound advice for today's angler. The author, Izaak Walton, introduced the idea of fishing purely for enjoyment and for experiencing the pleasure of being close to nature.

An umbrella keeps off the worst of the weather.

Fishing competitions

Competition fishing is very popular all over the world. National and even international matches attract thousands of anglers who compete for big prize money. The tackle that is used tends to be very light, so that hundreds of small fish can be landed within the time limits.

Great attention is paid to using bait and groundbait of the highest quality.

What is a fish?

FISH ARE WONDERFUL, delicate creatures and deserve all our respect. Their ability to see, hear, touch, and even smell is very well developed. Remember that when you approach the water's edge, fish will be able to sense you, hear you, and see you. Also, when you attach your bait, the fish will smell anything that is unpleasant or suspicious.

The world of fish
There are more than 20,000 known types of fish – mor than all mammals, birds, reptiles, and amphibians put together! They come in a variety of shapes and sizes, but all are uniquely adapted to their own environment.

The lateral line of a fish r along the centre of the body f the head to the tail. On mirror carp, it is l with big sc

Dorsal fin

Eye

Nostrils

Mouth

Lips

The gill flap, called the operculum, is a hard, bony area designed to give the fish maximum protection.

The pectoral fins are usually large to help produce bursts of speed.

A layer of slimy mucus protects against disease.

Pelvic fin

The anal fin is situated / down the body towards th tail and helps to stabilize the fish in a current.

Anatomy of a fish
The body of a fish is tightly packed with sensitive organs such as the heart, liver, swim-bladder, and stomach. Remember this when you hold a fish; if you squeeze it too tightly these organs will be crushed, the fish will feel pain, and it could even die.

The kidney is situated centrally, close to the backbone.

The brain coordinates all the fish's actions.

The eye may be large, especially in night feeders.

The delicate gills allow t fish to absor oxygen from the water.

Eggs are produced in the ovary.

Nutrients are absorbed into the blood via the intestines.

The heart pumps blood to the gills and around the body.

Swimming
Fish propel themselves through the water by pushing against it. Some do this by wriggling in a series of sideways curves, others move their tail area from side to side. This sequence shows the "S" shaped wave that passes along the body of a dogfish as it swims.

Note how the "S" shaped wave, which propels the fish through the water, is beginning to appear.

Pectoral fin

Pelvic fin

The dogfish swings its head to the right slightly to start the swimming movement.

The "peak" of the wave is now in the upper region of the fish between the pectoral and pelvic fins.

Living habits

Some fish live solitary lives, but most, especially small fish, live in large groups called shoals. Shoals are useful for defence. Big predators become confused when they see large numbers of fish break up and flee in panic. Shoal fish develop strong social instincts and, if the water is clear, you can even recognize leader fish, which dictate every movement.

Fish often like physical contact and will rub their bodies together.

Spawning brown trout lay their eggs in a hollow in the gravel.

Fish spawning

All fish spawn, or reproduce, in order to keep their populations alive. Different fish spawn at different times of the year. Salmon and trout spawn in the winter, whereas carp and most other bottom-feeding fish spawn as the water begins to warm up in the spring.

Life cycle

The transition from egg to fully grown fish is a very perilous one and only a fraction of the eggs laid even get as far as hatching out. This sequence shows the development of a young rainbow trout.

Blood vessels have already developed.

Eyes are clearly visible.

The fish is emerging.

1 After being laid, the fish's body starts to take shape within the transparent egg and its outline is clearly visible.

2 The young trout is nearly ready to hatch and can be seen moving about in the egg.

3 The fish has broken through the soft case of the egg and is preparing to wriggle out.

The young fish has plenty of food in its yolk sac when it hatches.

This rainbow-coloured band gives the rainbow trout its name.

The young trout has now hatched and is called an alevin. The yolk will gradually disappear.

At this stage, the young trout is called a parr.

5 Black stripes on the young trout's body have developed, giving it camouflage from predators.

6 The fully developed rainbow trout is a beautiful fish. The female will go on to lay thousands of eggs of her own over her breeding years.

Dorsal fin

Tail

Water will be displaced as the fish powers forward.

The snout of the fish moves to the right again and another "S" movement begins.

...wave has now moved further ...g the body and the fish is ...ding at the dorsal fin.

There is real power being produced now as the muscular movement reaches the hindquarters of the fish and the tail begins to thrust to the right.

This wave's peak finally reaches the tail and the fish is propelled forward.

Fish and their food

THERE IS AN OLD SAYING that sounds complicated, but it is quite true; the key to fishing is to put the right bait to the right fish at the right time in the right place in the right way! To get everything correct demands a real knowledge of the fish and, above all, you have got to know what your chosen quarry wants to eat. We have selected four of the world's most popular fish to show their different diets and ways of feeding.

Carp feed to a great extent by eyesight. Their vision is very good in clouded water and at night.

Carp
Of all fish, the carp probably has the most varied of diets and will eat virtually anything, from weed to dead fish. Although the mouth of the carp is toothless, the throat-teeth are incredibly strong and can crush the shells of mussels or crayfish.

Perch
The perch is a typical predator, for it likes to feed only on living organisms. When small, perch feed on worms and insects, but as soon as they reach 20 cm (8 in) or more in length, they move over to an almost exclusively fish diet. They also eat their own young.

The dorsal fin is held erect when hunting.

The distinctive stripes give the perch effective camouflage when mounting an ambush.

The tail fin is relatively small, so the perch relies on its body muscles for power.

The mouth is hinged, allowing it to open very wide to swallow large prey.

The sharp gill flap offers some protection against predators.

The stomach can hold prey one-third of its body weight.

The scales tend to be quite rough to the touch, especially just before spawning.

Sturgeon
The sturgeon is primarily a fish eater, but it can also uproot and devour creatures living in the bottom mud and slime. It uses its long, sharp nose to probe in the silt, looking for food. Its mouth can telescope open like a huge funnel and suck food in. A 4.5 kg (10 lb) carp or pike offers no problem to these fish, which can weigh over 136 kg (300 lb).

Most species have a bony ridge along the back. The armoured plates are called scutes.

The sturgeon's eyes are small, so it relies more on touch and smell when hunting.

The sturgeon uses its long whiskers to feel for food.

The mouth appears small, but it can telescope out to suck up food.

A bony lateral line runs along the length of the body.

The dorsal fin is raised when the carp swims quickly or is hungry. It is lowered when it rests.

These big scales give the fish some protection. They can be used to tell how long the fish has lived.

Mirror carp are recognized by their unique scale clusters, which are very much like our own fingerprints.

Carp are often deep-bodied. Big fish have massive appetites and can consume large amounts of food.

This huge tail fin gives the carp its amazing power.

...unfish

...nfish like water containing weed, as this is full of their ...vourite foods. The fish hunt for the larvae of insects, fish ..., and small molluscs. Most sunfish species eat snails and ... sometimes referred to as the "shell-crackers". Mayfly ...d stonefly larvae are ...so a favourite and ...nfish will even take ...ult flies that ...ve fallen ...to the ...ter.

The dorsal fin is held erect during feeding.

The tail is rounded in profile and fairly small.

...he mouth ...n open wide ... snatch ...rge insects.

A large eye helps the fish to home in on its prey.

The body stripes give the fish protection from bigger predators.

Large bottom fins give stability in the water.

The triangular dorsal fin is often seen cutting the surface of the water as the fish hunts.

The bony ridge continues along the top of the tail fin.

Eating habits

Fish have various ways of eating, depending on the shape of their mouth and their diet.

Seizing
The pike seizes its food. It approaches its prey with speed, opens its jaws, and sucks in the food with a rush of water. Then it clamps down hard with needle-sharp teeth.

Snatching
Many species, such as black bass, panfish, and trout will come to the surface to grab a land insect that has just entered their world. They will often do this violently with a splash.

Slurping
Carp slurp down food between extended lips. Floating baits are simply drawn down into the vortex the carp creates. Sometimes you will see bubbling and hear sucking sounds.

Sucking
Many fish, especially bottom feeders, suck up bait from the river-bed. They telescope out their lips, which creates a vacuum and allows water and food to be drawn into their mouths.

All kitted out

ALL YOU NEED when you start angling are some basic items. Tackle shops have a wide range of rods, reels, floats, leads, spinners, and hooks to choose from. Other essential items include warm clothes, an umbrella to keep off the rain, and a strong tackle box for all your equipment. A fold-up chair may come in handy too! However, try to avoid going to the waterside so laden down that you cannot keep mobile and search for new swims.

Your kit
Once you have collected your kit together, it is a very good idea to lay it all out before you go to the waterside. This helps you to familiarize yourself with everything and also allows you to check that you have not forgotten anything. Make sure you clean your tackle thoroughly after each outing and store it in a dry place.

Your first rod should be light and comfortable. Make sure you look after it.

There are lots of different seats on the market. Look for one that is easy to carry and fairly inexpensive. It should also be well made, so that it lasts.

A strong tackle box is essential to keep everything together.

You will need a rod rest if you are going bait fishing.

Catapult

Line

Reel

Bait box

Sunglasses

If you are thinking of going out in a boat to fish, then a life jacket is an absolute necessity, even if you are a strong swimmer.

Fish will eat almost anything that we eat, including cheese and spicy sausage!

You will need separate fly boxes for your dry and wet flies. Choose strong, sturdy boxes that close properly to prevent moisture from getting in.

Make sure you carry a selection of terminal tackle. This will allow you to present your bait properly in any type of weather or water condition.

Choose a hat with a broad brim when fishing in sunshine. This not only keeps the sun out of your eyes, but also helps you see more easily in bright light.

Although they are not strictly necessary, you will find that most experienced anglers use binoculars to scan the water for any sign of feeding fish.

Safety near water
You should always be aware of currents and hidden depths when you are near water. Look out for this symbol to indicate situations where you need to take extra care.

est waders

re is no doubt that
st waders give you
finite advantage
llowing you to get
e to the fish and
ent your bait
ny current. Never
yourself in danger
wading into areas
are unsure of.

*These waders
are made of
a special
breathable
fabric, so
you do not
get hot when
you walk.*

*Wear a number
of thin layers,
instead of one
thick one.*

*Most thigh
boots are made
out of rubber.*

Thigh waders

For fishing in shallow waters,
thigh waders are ideal. Choose
a light pair, with a good grip
on the soles and lightweight
uppers that can be folded down
to transform the waders into
boots. Again, always be sure
you stay in your depth.

Handy gloves

It is important to keep warm
while you are fishing, otherwise
it will be difficult to concentrate
and you will want to go home.
As your fingers and toes often
feel the cold first, thick socks
and gloves are a good idea.

*This slit is useful
for feeling the line.*

These gloves are made of
a special material called
Neoprene, which is very
warm and water-resistant.

*The thumb and
finger pieces
fold back.*

These fold-back fingertips
allow you to tie knots or bait
the hook quickly and easily –
and still keep warm!

*Choose your
footwear carefully.
Look for a good
grip and some
waterproofing.*

*Your rod is a
very precious
item, so always
store it in a
protective bag or
case after you have
used it. Clean it
thoroughly after
each trip to make
it last longer.*

*Choose a soft mesh
or your landing net
because this is kinder
n the fish. Whenever
ossible, keep the net in the
water as you unhook the fish.*

*A selection of floats
to suit all water
conditions*

*A tub of split shot is
essential, especially if
you are float fishing.*

Tackle box

A tackle box like this one can hold an
enormous amount of gear, providing
you pack it carefully! Plan what you are
going to put on each of the different
levels and try to stick to it. The clear lid
lets you see everything in its place.

Fishing tackle

THE EQUIPMENT you will need will vary according to whether you want to fish mainly in freshwater or saltwater. Look for reliable tackle that is fairly inexpensive. It is especially important to choose the right lines and hooks, because if they fail you, the fish will be lost. You will find that most tackle dealers are happy to spend time advising you, as they know that a contented customer will always return.

Spinning rod

Most spinning rods are fairly short so you can work those intriguing areas under low-lying trees. The screw fitting on the reel seat stops the reel working loose during repeated casting.

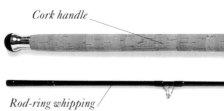

Cork handle

Rod-ring whipping

The reel spool is filled nearly to the brim with line.

Coarse-fishing reel

The fixed-spool reel is used for all types of bait fishing. It is very easy to cast with and modern varieties have reliable clutches to allow you to give line to running fish.

Fly rod

The fly rod is a delicate wand of a tool. Choose one that feels comfortable and you should be able to fish all day without tiring.

Reel seat

Fly-fishing reel

Compared with a fixed-spool reel, a fly-fishing reel tends to be quite simple and straightforward. Check that the reel has an adjustable clutch.

Flies

There are literally thousands of fly patterns around the world, but in general you should aim to fish dry flies on the surface, nymphs towards the bottom, and streamer-type flies quickly through mid-water.

Dry fly

Mini-lure

Fly imitation

The holes let water drain from the line.

Imitation shrimp

Imitation caddis

Streamer fly

The feathers move in the water.

The blade revolves on the surface.

Top-water plug

Plugs

There are lots of different types of pl[u]... from those that float on the surface to those that bounce along the bottom. Colour is also very important – go for light, even neon colours if the water i[s] cloudy, or subdued colours if it is cle[ar]. Always take a selection with you.

Surface plug

Floats

There are differently shaped floats for still- and running water (see pages 28–29), so check carefully that you have the right floats with you for the day's fishing ahead. If in doubt, choose a heavier float, as this will always give you more control over the prevailing conditions.

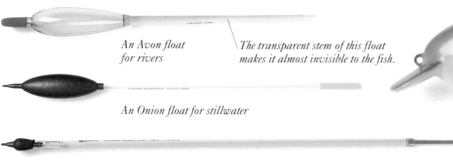

An Avon float for rivers

The transparent stem of this float makes it almost invisible to the fish.

An Onion float for stillwater

A loaded waggler for stillwater

Shallow diver

This type of lure will send lots of vibrations through the water.

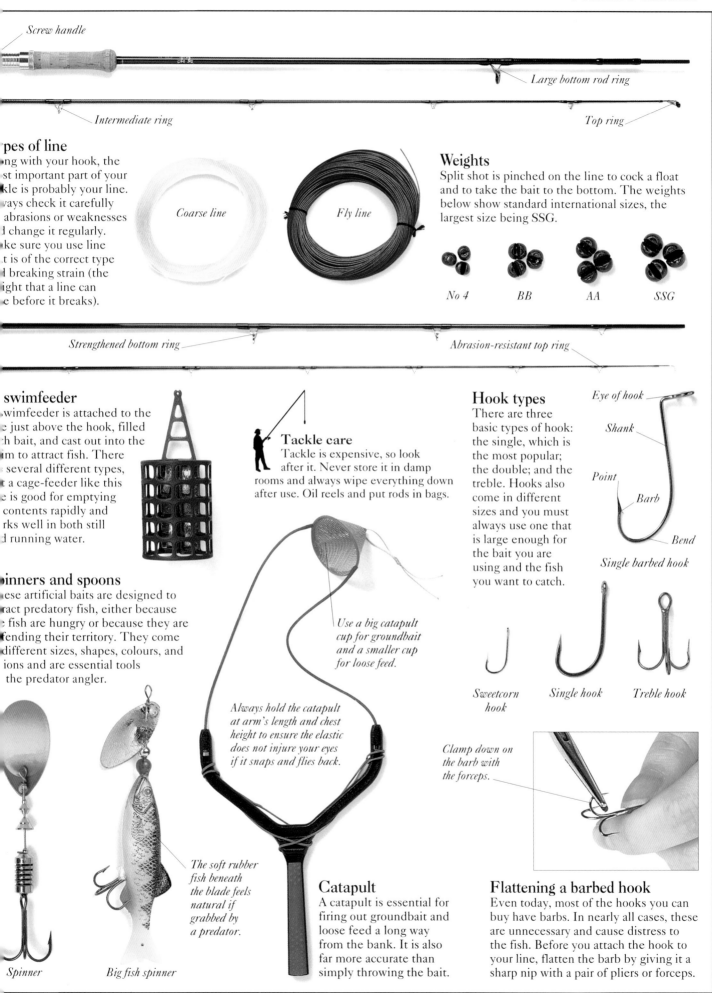

Screw handle

Large bottom rod ring

Intermediate ring

Top ring

Types of line

Along with your hook, the most important part of your tackle is probably your line. Always check it carefully for abrasions or weaknesses and change it regularly. Make sure you use line that is of the correct type and breaking strain (the weight that a line can take before it breaks).

Coarse line

Fly line

Weights

Split shot is pinched on the line to cock a float and to take the bait to the bottom. The weights below show standard international sizes, the largest size being SSG.

No 4   *BB*   *AA*   *SSG*

Strengthened bottom ring

Abrasion-resistant top ring

Swimfeeder

A swimfeeder is attached to the line just above the hook, filled with bait, and cast out into the swim to attract fish. There are several different types, but a cage-feeder like this one is good for emptying its contents rapidly and works well in both still and running water.

Tackle care

Tackle is expensive, so look after it. Never store it in damp rooms and always wipe everything down after use. Oil reels and put rods in bags.

Spinners and spoons

These artificial baits are designed to attract predatory fish, either because the fish are hungry or because they are defending their territory. They come in different sizes, shapes, colours, and actions and are essential tools for the predator angler.

Use a big catapult cup for groundbait and a smaller cup for loose feed.

Always hold the catapult at arm's length and chest height to ensure the elastic does not injure your eyes if it snaps and flies back.

The soft rubber fish beneath the blade feels natural if grabbed by a predator.

Spinner   *Big fish spinner*

Catapult

A catapult is essential for firing out groundbait and loose feed a long way from the bank. It is also far more accurate than simply throwing the bait.

Hook types

There are three basic types of hook: the single, which is the most popular; the double; and the treble. Hooks also come in different sizes and you must always use one that is large enough for the bait you are using and the fish you want to catch.

Eye of hook

Shank

Point

Barb

Bend

Single barbed hook

Sweetcorn hook   *Single hook*   *Treble hook*

Clamp down on the barb with the forceps.

Flattening a barbed hook

Even today, most of the hooks you can buy have barbs. In nearly all cases, these are unnecessary and cause distress to the fish. Before you attach the hook to your line, flatten the barb by giving it a sharp nip with a pair of pliers or forceps.

Getting ready to fish

AT FIRST SIGHT, the amount of fishing tackle that you need can seem pretty daunting. However, do not worry. After just a very few trips, you'll get used to what everything does and how to assemble it in a quick, easy way. Concentrate on getting good quality, basic kit that you are happy with and can trust in every situation; the more advanced items can come later.

1 Make sure that the ends of the pieces to be joined are quite clean. Push them together until you feel the fit is absolutely secure.

A light spinning rod like this one is perfect for catching small pike and perch.

Attaching a reel

1 Push the seat of the reel firmly into the grip, which is situated on the rod butt.

2 Make sure it fits snugly and check the reel is facing up the rod and not back to front!

3 Once the reel is screwed in tightly, start to push back the bale arm to begin casting.

4 Hold the line tight once you have released the bale arm.

Putting the rod together

Some rods are just one piece, but most come in two or three lengths that have to be joined together. When you first start fishing, use a 3 m (9 ft) rod.

Lower the rod to help you put the line through the top rings.

Make sure you keep the rod rings clean by wiping them occasionally with a cloth and some soapy water. Replace worn or cracked rings.

2 Look down the rod to make sure the rings are all lined up correctly. This is extremely important. If they are not, you will find casting much more difficult.

3 With the bale arm of the reel open, pull the line off the reel and thread it through the rings. Watch out for tangles around the reel handle.

Grip the hook firmly between the thumb and index finger of your left hand.

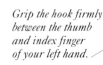

4 Once the reel is safely on the rod and the line is through the rings, shut the reel bale arm and begin to put the tackle and bait on the end of the line.

Make sure the bale arm is open as you thread the line through the rings.

The ideal location
Now for the really hard part – the moment you turn fishing detective. Both stillwaters and rivers can look very large, forbidding places at first. Where do you start? Do not rush in and set up your gear at the first available place. Spend time walking around the water looking for any signs of fish or for the places you think they might be hiding, such as reeds, islands, and lily pads.

Tying a half-blood knot

Every angler needs to know how to tie a basic, secure knot. There are many different types, which can be bewildering at first. However, it is possible to use just one type of knot for attaching hooks, spinners, and whatever else you will need throughout your angling career – the half-blood knot.

Preventing friction
To prevent a knot from slipping, wet it with water. This will reduce any friction that might occur and will prevent the line from being damaged.

1 Push about 15 cm (6 in) of line through the hook eye. Make a big loop and put the spare end under the main line.

2 Use your right hand to keep the loop open and with your left hand, move the line anti-clockwise around the loose end.

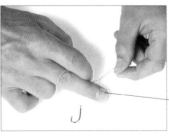

3 Repeat this anti-clockwise movement about five times. Use your finger to keep the loop above the hook open.

Remember to keep your fingers clear of the hook point.

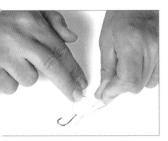

4 Push the end of the spare line through the open loop with your left hand. Hold the loop firmly in your right hand.

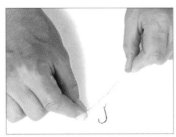

5 Start to tighten the knot, using your left hand to pull the main line and your right hand to pull the spare line.

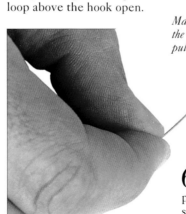

Make sure the knot is pulled tight.

6 The knot forms above the eye of the hook as you keep pulling. Use scissors to trim spare line close to the loop.

Basic casting

WHEN YOU CAST, you simply use your rod and reel to flick the line, tackle, and bait out into the water where the fish will find it. It is one of the most essential skills in fishing, because you are not going to catch anything on the bank! However, it is important not to be put off by the techniques involved in casting. Modern tackle has made casting much easier and you should be able to master it in a few sessions.

Basic technique

Before you begin the casting action, make sure you are standing in a comfortable position. Aim to make the cast a smooth, unhurried motion. The rod, reel, and line should do all the work for you. When you first begin casting, concentrate on accuracy rather than distance. Try to get your bait to land exactly where you want it to, especially if you have put some groundbait in to attract the fish to one particular area. It is worth practising at home with a bucket as a target. This will save time at the riverbank.

If your rod is too far back as the casting begins, at nine o'clock for example, you will lose some control.

A peaked cap will shade your eyes from the sun.

Move smoothly so the line does not tangle.

Try to keep the rod as steady as possible.

Stand with your feet apart.

1 Look to where you want to cast. Trap the line against the reel stem with your finger, then move the bale arm over with your left hand.

2 Still with your eyes on the target area, begin to move the rod backwards. Slide your left hand down to the butt of the rod.

3 Watch your tackle to ensure it does not tangle as you move the rod over your shoulder. Let your bait hang about 1 m (3 ft) beneath the rod tip.

4 Wait for your tackle to settle as it hangs over your shoulder. Pause to make sure that everything is tangle-free before making the all-important cast.

The correct grip

It is important that you get used to handling the basic equipment as soon as possible. Put the rod and reel together at the tackle shop before you make any purchase. Buy a reel that is the right size for you, or you will find that your fingers have difficulty stretching to the reel's controls and line.

Bale arm

Move the bale arm over until it is fully open. You will probably hear a click that will tell you this action is complete.

1 Hold the rod in your right hand. The bale arm should be closed.

4 You are now ready to cast. Hold the line tight while the rod is going through the casting arc (see below) and don't let it go off too early.

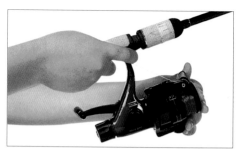

2 Take the line from the reel and trap it under your index finger. Start to move the bale arm with the other hand.

5 Once your rod has moved to the one o'clock position, you can release the line, allowing the terminal tackle to shoot out.

Not too tight!
Allow the main weight that you are casting to swing about 1 m (3 ft) from the rod tip. Any more or less, and you could get into a terrible tangle.

Keep your finger clear of the flying line.

Keep your feet apart and your body balanced throughout the cast.

Now, in one quick, smooth movement, bring the rod over your shoulder to the two o'clock position, lifting your finger to let the line fly out as you do so.

When the cast is finished, wind the reel handle to engage the bale arm and you are ready to start fishing.

6 Finish the cast off with the rod held somewhere between two and three o'clock. Don't go too low or the bait will land with a fish-frightening splash!

The clock face
The positions on the clock face are used to describe the rod movements during casting. At the start of casting (stage 4), your rod should be pointing to ten o'clock. At one o'clock, you will be letting the line go with your finger. The cast is over when the rod is between two and three o'clock.

Fly fishing

THE MAJOR CONCERN of most young anglers when fly fishing is how to cast. Do not worry, all you need to master is the basic overhead cast, as it is the basis of all the other cast forms. You can learn fly casting in a few hours – try practising at home on the lawn. Remember, presenting the right fly in the right place is much more important than straining to cast at the horizon.

A *dry fly floats on the surface to attract a rising fish.*

Choosing a fly
Watch the water carefully and if you see rings, indicating that the fish is rising, try a dry fly. If there is no surface activity, start with a nymph pattern.

The ideal location
This picture shows the perfect spot for fly fishing. The water runs quickly over the gravel, then deepens slightly and slows down. Trout and grayling especially love this clean, well-oxygenated water, and their favourite food lives among the stones on the river-bed.

Fly rod
Fly rods tend to be light and responsive and you should be able to handle one all day without tiring. The reel sits right at the bottom of the rod for better balance.

Fly casting
The overhead cast entails lifting the line off the water and sending it straight out behind you. This is called the back cast and the weight of the shooting line bends the rod and gives it its power. Once the line is fully extended, you then move the rod forward and the line whistles through the air to place the fly on the water before you. Practice will very soon make perfect.

Wade carefully
Never wade so far out that you put yourself in danger. Remember that even in shallow water, the current can still be very swift and strong.

Hold the rod firmly in your casting hand, well above the reel.

1 Lift the line off the water and begin the back cast. Try to lift the line off in one smooth, continuous motion, keeping your wrist fairly straight. Do not be timid and put plenty of power into the action.

Make sure your rod stops about the ten o'clo position on you back cast.

2 It is a good idea to look over your shoulder to see what the line is doing. the line straighten out before you begin t forward cast. Don't let your rod fall too lo behind you and keep the line off the ban

Tread carefully
Walk slowly into the river
as the sound of crunching
gravel may frighten the fish.

*Keep your hand, wrist, and rod
in a straight line and hold the
rod firmly, so that the rod
nestles in your forearm.*

*Always wear protective
glasses when you are
fly fishing to protect
against stray flies.*

*Retrieve the
line slowly
and carefully
in the fingers
of your non-
casting hand.*

*Vary the retrieve to make the fly
look as realistic as possible.*

After completing the forward cast, the line shoots through the
rod rings and places the fly on the water a good way beyond
. To avoid a splashy cast, aim your fly at a spot about 1m (3 ft)
ve the surface. Don't let your rod tip drop too close to the
er or you will find that the line goes down in an untidy heap.

4 As you retrieve your fly, watch out for any sign of a take.
Sometimes you will feel a tug, but on other occasions you will
simply see your fly line either pause or shoot forward a couple of
inches. Strike at once. When the fly is about 5 m (16 ft) away from
you, move again into your next back cast.

Flies in action

T HE REAL SKILL of fly fishing is knowing exactly what the fish are feeding on in the natural world. You can then attempt to imitate the real insect with an artificial one. To master this skill, you will need to watch the water very carefully and build up a picture of how the fish are behaving at different times of the day. This may sound difficult, but it is a fascinating way to fish.

Watching the water

It is very important to keep a low profile and avoid frightening the fish at all costs. Approach stealthily, and try to get as close to them as possible.

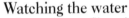

Surface feeding

One of the most exciting sights for an angler is a trout coming up to sip flies from the surface. Sometimes this will a splashy movement at other times you'll just hear a slurp and see the fish's nose. Try to identify the natural fly being taken and present one of your own flies to look as near to the real thing as possible. Heart-stopping stuff

Artificial mayflies

Compared with other flies, mayflies are very large and therefore fairly easy to present to the trout in a convincing way.

Grey Wulff

The real thing

Swarms of adult mayflies are found near rivers throughout the summer. Often called "dayflies" because their lives are so short, mayflies die after mating.

Cut-wing green Drake

Closing in!

There is not a more exciting sight in the whole of angling than to watch a trout moving in on your fly – either above or below the surface. Often, a trout will get very close to the fly and even follow it for a while before making a decision. Sometimes it pays to stop retrieving and let the fly sink a little in the water. Other times, it is better to speed up and perhaps lift the fly to the surface, so that the trout thinks it is escaping and makes an instant decision to take it!

Wet flies

Traditional wet flies give the impression of food, rather than actually imitating something. Flies such as the Butcher are tied to attract the trout's attention as they move through quick water.

Butcher

Soldier Palmer

Nymphing for trout

The word "nymphing" actually describes presenting the trout with small flies, which represent very common items on their daily menu. These items include the nymphs or larval stages of flies, as well as other small aquatic creatures, such as tiny beetles, snails, and shrimps. Fish them slowly and carefully.

Trout love water shrimps.

This artificial shrimp looks very like the real thing.

Shrimp

Gammarus water shrimp

Here, my Polaroid glasses give me an excellent view of what is happening in the trout's kingdom.

Freshwater shrimps

Freshwater shrimps cannot survive in polluted water, so their presence is a sure sign that the water is clean. Make sure that your imitation shrimps are weighted well.

Nymphs

Mayfly nymphs live for about a year underwater. They are a favourite food of trout. Imitation nymphs should look like small, dark food items so that they do not arouse suspicion. Move them slowly through the water with small jerks.

Mayfly nymph

Marabou nymph

Lure fishing

Lure FISHING is one of the most exciting ways of catching predatory fish. Pike, perch, zander, trout . . . there is an endless list of fish that will gobble these plastic, metal, or wood creations, mistaking them for real fish. There are three types of lure. Spinners and spoons are usually made of metal and either wobble or spin through the water in the same way as a real fish. Plugs are made of wood or plastic and work in a number of ways: along the surface of the water, in mid-water, or deep along the bottom.

The ideal location
When you are lure fishing, it pays to search the water and not stay too long in any one position. A spot like this is ideal – big predators like slack water just off the main current, and some often lie close in to the bank.

Always use a wire trace if you think that pike are present, as their sharp teeth cut through nylon.

Attention to detail
Predatory fish are eagle-eyed and a good plug should resemble a natural fish very closely. Look for realistic eyes, scale patterns, and a shiny finish.

Make sure that the hooks on your lure are strong enough for the fish you want to catch.

Lure rod
The ideal lure rod is light, but with some power to give you control over a big fish. Look for a rod about 3 m (9 ft) long.

Careful approach
Predatory fish are extremely wary, so approach the water carefully or you might scare the fish before you have even started!

Working a lure
Never work your spoon, spinner, or plug in a mechanical, unthinking sort of way. Instead, aim to make a big predator think that this strange wood, metal, or plastic creation is in fact a living, breathing, swimming prey fish! Look out for all possible hidey-holes under fallen trees, among weeds, or tucked in close to the bank. Cast carefully and accurately and constantly move the rod tip around to create a change of direction.

1 Make sure that your lure is swinging about 1m (3 ft) from your rod tip before you begin to cast. It is a good idea to have a quick look at the lure to check that it is fairly still before you begin. Also look closely at where you want the lure to land. Make sure you are standing comfortably and safely and then begin the cast.

Search out the edge of the current, as well as slack water.

The clutch on your reel should be precisely set so that it will give line to a big running fish.

Watch the river and the lure as it flies out across the water. As the lure approaches your chosen spot, slow down the line with your fingers so that it lands exactly where you want it to. Work the lure close to the surface. Let it stop sometimes as though it is resting, then quickly jerk it across the water as though it is in a panic and trying to escape from a predator it has just spotted.

3 Very often, predators will follow a lure right to the bank before deciding to attack. If you move the lure out too quickly, there is every chance you will snatch it from the jaws of the fish. So watch the lure very carefully until it is right at your feet, before lifting it out of the water. Stand a little way back from the riverbank, to avoid being spotted by any approaching predator.

Lures in action

ONE OF THE REAL SKILLS of lure fishing is to know exactly which type of lure – spinner, spoon, or plug – to use in any given situation. To get the best out of this type of fishing, you should keep moving around the river or lake, looking for all manner of underwater obstructions and water features that will attract fish. Each area will demand a slightly different approach and lure, which is why it is important to build up a collection of lures. You can then experiment with different depths and techniques. Always make your lure look as lifelike as possible.

The ideal location
Search out any areas that might offer a predator good ambush opportunities. Fish such as pike and perch like to wait near reed beds, close to weeds, or beneath overhanging trees, where they a almost invisible to shoals of passing prey fish.

Fish awareness
The use of treble hooks on lures can sometimes be dangerous to the fish if they are in an aggressive taking mood. Always try to use a spoon with just a single hook and ensure that the barb has been flattened for easy removal.

The Hunter is a pike lure, designed to be fished slowly just off the bottom.

The Stingfish dives rapidly when it is reeled in quickly.

The Heddon Torpedo is a surface lure.

This propeller churns up the water when retrieved.

Plugs
A plug is designed to look and move in the same way as a small p fish, which often swims in distress. Plugs can be used for any dep of water. Work them slowly in areas that might contain big preda

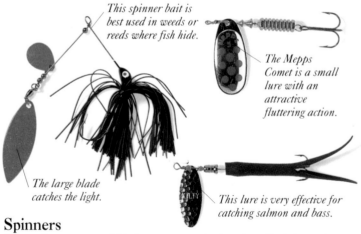

This spinner bait is best used in weeds or reeds where fish hide.

The Mepps Comet is a small lure with an attractive fluttering action.

The large blade catches the light.

This lure is very effective for catching salmon and bass.

Spinners
On a spinner, a metal blade rotates as the lure is pulled through the water. This sends out vibrations and catches the light so that it looks just like a small fish. Sometimes tassels of plastic or wool are added to entice the fish further.

Down she goes!
This pike has taken a lure fished close to the surface and is now plunging towards the bottom in an attempt to escape. Keep pressure on the fish and do not let it get into any underwater sna – you do not want to leave a fish with hooks in its mouth.

A leaping bass

Many fish, like this bass, will immediately jump out of the water when they are hooked. Drop your rod tip just a little to slacken pressure on the line, otherwise you might find that it breaks. This is a dangerous moment, because the hooks can easily be thrown free.

This bass is perfectly hooked in the lip.

The Heron is a king-sized lure used for catching pike.

The Atlantic spoon is very effective when fished slowly.

The rippled finish of the Abu Atom catches and reflects the light as it is pulled through the water.

Spoons

A spoon is a lure made of shaped sheet metal. When cast and retrieved from the bank, spoons wobble through the water and attract predatory fish with their shiny finish and bright colours. Their action depends on the style of retrieve, so wind in erratically to make them look like a fish in distress.

ur quarry

re fishing is perfect for all manner of dators. In general, the smaller the fish, smaller the lure you should use. For mple, a Mepps Comet lure would be fect for this perch (right) but for really fish, like pike, you should move up in e and use the Heron or the Stingfish. ok for signs in the water to help you ide which lure to use. For example, rey fish are showering out of the water, will know a hunter is at work. If there no signs, you will need to observe ry feature in the water very carefully. ink out each cast. Change the speed etrieve. Move your rod tip around so lure follows different tracks through water. In cold weather, try to fish eep as possible – you actually feel r spinner or spoon bounce along the tom, where the big fish are lying.

Bait fishing

I T IS VERY IMPORTANT to make sure that your bait is in tiptop condition. Wary fish will not accept old or stale bait. Whatever you use, it should have an appealing aroma. It should also look fresh; a live, wriggling worm is far more attractive than a dead one. Make sure that your bait is on the right-sized hook. It is no good having a huge bait on a tiny hook or vice-versa. Never be afraid to go for an unusual bait. Fish wise-up quickly, so something out of the ordinary may well fool them.

Getting the bait down
Most fish will take bait that is lying on the bottom, so you have to g both the hook bait and any loose bait down there quickly. Swimfee and bait droppers both accomplish this task. Pack the feeder tightl cast it out, and it will release its load of bait on the bed.

A huge variety
There are many types of bait and some, like these "particle baits", need boiling to soften them. They are small and plentiful, encouraging fish to feed in a frenzy so that they suck up the bait without inspecting it properly.

These high-protein (HP) baits are called boilies and are made of milk proteins, eggs, soy flour, wheatgerm, animal proteins, flavourings, and colourings.

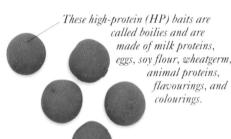

Cooked butter beans   *Cooked haricot be*

Cooked pasta   *Cooked chickpeas*   *Cooked dried peas*

Peanuts   *Raw tares*

Cooked tares   *Processed hemp*   *Cooked maize*   *Cooked rice*

Baits from the kitchen
Some of the most useful baits can be found in the kitchen cupboard or fridge. However, ask permission before disappearing with the evening meal!

Bread
Use bread that is as fresh as possible. Push the hook through a small piece and squeeze tightly around the shank. The rest should remain fluffy so it expands in the water.

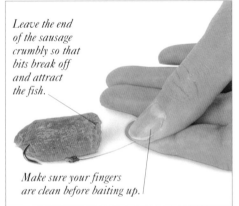

Leave the end of the sausage crumbly so that bits break off and attract the fish.

Make sure your fingers are clean before baiting up.

Sausage
There are many types of ready-cooked sausage available today – just look at the range in your local supermarket. Sausages make excellent baits because fish can smell their strong aroma even in cloudy water conditions. Cut a suitable length of sausage and thread the hook through. Make sure the hook point stands proud of any tough skin.

Push the hook deep inside the corn so that it does not fly off when casting.

A golden hook can often fool suspicious fish.

Sweetcorn
Nearly all fish adore the tiny, sweet, yellow grains of sweetcorn. Use corn that is as fresh and sugary as possible. You can thread one grain on to a small hook, or five or six grains on to a bigger hook for large fish. Try varying the size of the hook and the number of grains if you are not getting any bites.

Natural baits

...me of the best baits are also the simplest, such ...hose that you find in and around the water. ...er all, this is what the fish are used to eating ...ry day and their suspicions are unlikely to be ...used. The other advantage is that baits that ...u find around you are free!

...u can dig your ...n lugworms at ... tide on the ...dflats. However, ...ke sure that the tide ...n the way out first.

All sorts of mussels are good for catching both freshwater and sea fish. Do not use them if the water has limited stocks.

The predator

For big, aggressive predators like pike, you cannot beat fresh fish, their natural food. Try using dead sea fish as baits; sprats, herrings, mackerel, and sardines all make excellent deadbaits for pike. Small freshwater fish also work well, especially those with silvery scales.

Other good baits include leeches, all types of nymph, freshwater shrimps, and small snails.

The river larder

For chub, barbel, roach, dace, and a host of other river species you cannot do better than use the sort of foodstuffs you find under any largish stone or rock. Probably the best bait is the caddis grub that makes a little cocoon for itself. Ease the shell off the rock and gently prize the grub out of its cover. Two caddis grubs on a fairly small hook are perfect bait for both legered and float fish.

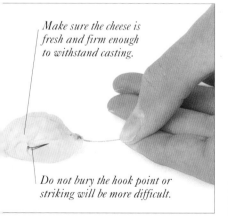

Make sure the cheese is fresh and firm enough to withstand casting.

Do not bury the hook point or striking will be more difficult.

Cheese

...eese is another excellent bait for murky ...ter conditions when visibility is low. ...amy cheeses are especially good if they ...mixed with dry bread. Knead the two ...ether until you get a firm paste that ...ks to the hook and stays there during ...ting. Most species love mouldy cheese, ...do not be afraid of using smelly leftovers.

Float fishing

FLOATS CAN BE MADE of quill, wood, cork, or plastic. You can use a float to fish bait at various depths, from just under the surface of the water, to right on the bottom. If you are fishing a river you can try trotting a bait under a float, which means allowing it to move with the current. Most importantly, a float gives you an immediate bite indication so that you can strike early and not deep hook your fish.

A float rod
The ideal float rod should be around 3–4 m (10–13 ft) long, light enough to allow use of comparatively light lines, and comfortable enough to hold all day. It should also have a flexible tip section.

Use brightly coloured float tips in dark, shaded waters.

Use enough shot to pull the float down so that only the tip is visible.

The ideal location
A deepish channel close to an island is a perfect float-fishing location. Fish will funnel through areas like this as they move around the lake. Choppy water helps to hide your float from the eyes of wary fish.

Finding the depth
Start fishing your bait close to the surface, then move it closer and closer to the bottom until you find where the fish are feeding.

A piece of sweetcorn next to a maggot makes an appetizing bait cocktail!

Make sure your maggots are fresh and lively and replace them frequently.

Float fishing
It is important to choose the right float for the job. On a stillwater, a straight-bodied waggler-type float is perfect. Use one that is heavy enough to cast easily and is clearly visible, even at a distance in rough water.

Hold the end of the line firmly, leaving a few centimetres standing proud of your fingers.

1 Thread the line carefully through all of the rod rings. Always put the line through the centre of the eye. Leave the bale arm of the reel open so that the line comes off the spool easily. Take care that the line does not loop off too early and get tangled.

Make sure the attachment ring is clear of varnish so that the line passes through easily.

2 When you're fishing a stillwater, attach just the bottom end of the float to the line. Wind the line through the bottom ring a couple of times so that it hangs secure in position. Alternatively, you can secure the float by placing shot above and below it.

Reading the bites

Every fish bites differently, giving different indications on the float. Strike too soon, and you will miss the fish, strike too late and the bait may be swallowed. As a rule of thumb, always strike early. If you are missing bites, delay a second or so each time until you begin to hook the fish. As your experience grows, your timing will get better and better.

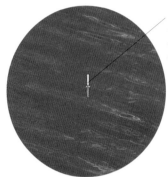

The float tip is brightly coloured for easy visibility.

The correct setting
The float is just visible above the water line. It is correctly shotted so that any movement will be detected at once. The shot rests on the bottom of the pool and the bait is about 15 cm (6 in) away.

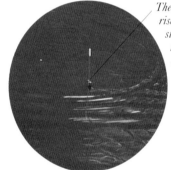

The float will rise slowly and steadily when the bottom shot is lifted.

Taking the bait
As a small carp or tench takes and sucks at the bait, the shot that has cocked the float is lifted. The float itself begins to rise in the water. Do not strike yet because the fish is still mouthing the bait.

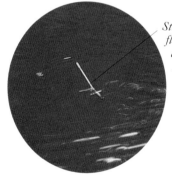

Strike before the float begins to dip under the surface of the water.

The right time to strike
The float teeters at a 45° angle to the water as the fish moves away with the bait in its mouth. Strike now, before the fish feels the weight of the shot and spits out the bait.

...en casting, look ...efully at the spot on ...water you want the ...at to settle in.

Hold the rod steady over your head before casting.

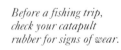

Before a fishing trip, check your catapult rubber for signs of wear.

...Hold the rod vertically over your shoulder in line with the area of water ...u want to cast towards. Move the rod ...oothly and powerfully. Once the rod ...n the two o'clock position in front of ...u, let the line fly out. Keep your finger ...se to the spool of the reel so you can ...p the line when the float has reached ...e right place.

4 Scatter loose feed around your float with a catapult. This is more accurate than throwing the bait by hand as it allows you to position bait at greater distances. The smell of the feed should draw the fish out into the open water. Do not overdo the bait. Start with a small amount and increase it gradually if you are getting lots of bites.

Legering

LEGERING IS PLACING a bait on the bottom of the river or lake that you are fishing, usually with some sort of lead to hold it in place. It is particularly useful when you are hoping to ambush a big fish and you need to keep the bait in the same position for a fairly long period. There is no float to indicate when you have a bite, so other forms of indication are needed to avoid ending up with a deeply hooked fish.

The rod

At about 3 m (9 ft) in length, legering rods tend to be shorter than float rods. Try to match the strength of the rod with the power and size of the fish.

The ideal location

This is a perfect spot for legering. The thick rushes at the far en of the lake are superb habitat for all types of bottom feeders and the angler can sit a little bit back from the water's edge, well screened by the long grasses.

Using a bobbin

A bobbin indicator is a very easy and efficient way of determining whether you have a bite. The bobbin can either be a piece of bread, a cork, or a cylinder of silver foil tied to the line between the first and second rod rings. The bobbin will move when a fish takes the bait.

Night legering
A small glowing isotope instead of a piece of bread shines brightly on a dark night.

2 Wait until you see the bobbin moving either up or down in a positive manner and then strike! It is important to time your bite correctly, because if you wait too long, the fish will either drop the bait or be deeply hooked.

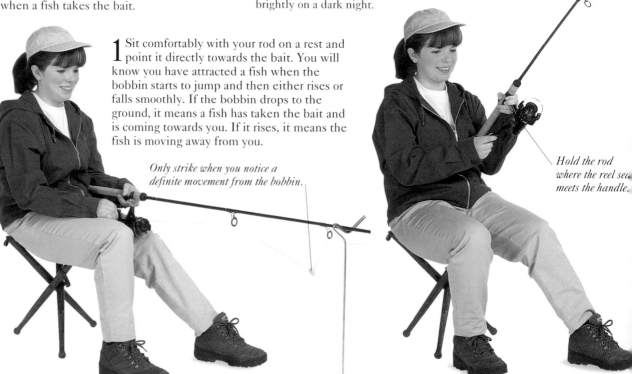

1 Sit comfortably with your rod on a rest and point it directly towards the bait. You will know you have attracted a fish when the bobbin starts to jump and then either rises or falls smoothly. If the bobbin drops to the ground, it means a fish has taken the bait and is coming towards you. If it rises, it means the fish is moving away from you.

Only strike when you notice a definite movement from the bobbin.

Hold the rod where the reel sea meets the handle.

...uivertipping

...en fishing a river, it is a good
...a to use a quivertip to indicate
...es. A quivertip is a very fine
...ce of carbon inserted into the
...d of a normal rod, and it is very
...sitive to any biting fish.
...ivertips come in a variety of
...gths and strengths, all made
...match the power of the river
...the weight of the lead you
...using. Look for a tip painted
...and/or white, as this makes it
...y visible against the sky or
...kground trees. A bite can
...er be a series of trembles or
...ocks on the tip, but sometimes
...tip will slam around, leaving
...in no doubt at all.

*...gentle curve
...his legering rod
...erfect for
...fish.*

*Line up your tip against any
light background, so that it is
easier to watch over a long
period of time.*

*Keep your grip
relaxed and easy.*

1 Place the quivertip where you can clearly see it, such as
against an area of white water. Try to get just a slight bend
in the quivertip – if it is too acute, you will not be able to
make out the action of a biting fish.

2 Position yourself on the bank so
that you are ready to spring into
action the instant you see a bite
indicated on the quivertip. Always
try to travel light, so that if you are
unsuccessful in one spot, you can
move on to try another.

...atching the bite

...ke sure that the bread you use for your bread
...licator is as fresh as possible so that it clings to the
...e. You can alter the size of the bobbin according to
...wind and current. In very calm conditions, when
...re is little or no undertow, a small bobbin will be
...quate. In rougher weather conditions, you will
...d to use a larger, heavier bobbin. Make sure the
...bbin hangs steadily beneath the rod.

1 Before you cast,
decide where you
want to fish. If you are
fishing close to the
bank, you can just swing
the bait out into the
water with an underarm
movement. For longer
distances, you will need
an overhead cast and a
heavier bobbin.

Touch legering

Touch legering is the most sensitive way of feeling for a bite, especially on
a river. It is very exciting because you actually feel the fish nosing your
bait, taking the hook, and swimming away with it. This is a straightforward
technique and the only equipment you need is your fingers!

2 Once you have
completed the cast,
you can simply tighten
up and place the
bobbin on your line
between the bottom
two rod rings. Keep
your hand on the rod
butt and watch the
bobbin carefully for
any signs of activity.

*Hold your rod comfortably
and pointing towards the
bait. Then pull the line away
near the reel and just slip it
around your fingers, so that
you can sense any tugs the
second you get a bite.*

Shore fishing

CASTING FROM THE SHORE into surf is one of the most physical forms of angling. Correct technique rather than brute force is the key, otherwise you will spoil your body action. Study the basic movements shown below and build up a good, smooth rhythm. You will find that your casting distances will gradually increase with practice.

The ideal location
Shore fishing is not always about casting long distances. Where you have rocks and cliffs, you will find that many fish species such as bass and wrasse will come in very close.

Safety near water
Always watch out for an incoming tide. Never risk being cut off by the rising water.

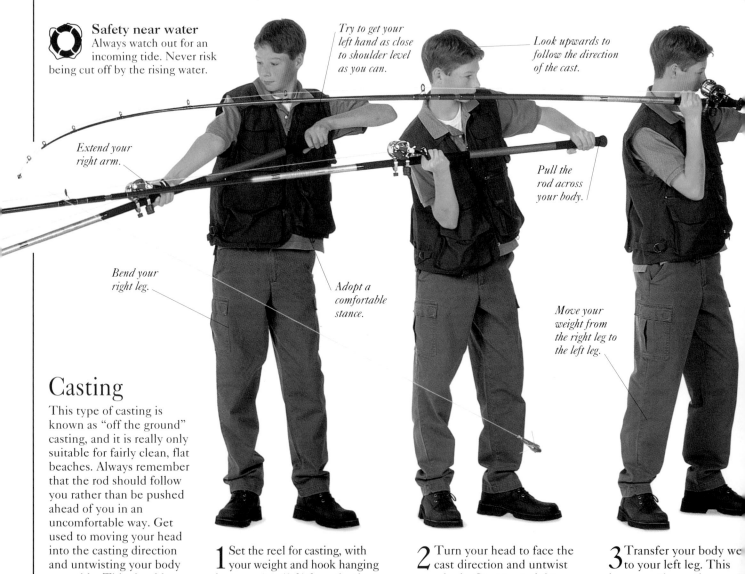

Try to get your left hand as close to shoulder level as you can.

Look upwards to follow the direction of the cast.

Extend your right arm.

Pull the rod across your body.

Bend your right leg.

Adopt a comfortable stance.

Move your weight from the right leg to the left leg.

Casting

This type of casting is known as "off the ground" casting, and it is really only suitable for fairly clean, flat beaches. Always remember that the rod should follow you rather than be pushed ahead of you in an uncomfortable way. Get used to moving your head into the casting direction and untwisting your body smoothly. This should all become one fluid movement when you have practised it enough.

1 Set the reel for casting, with your weight and hook hanging just over 1 m (3 ft) from the tip ring. Put your thumb over the line. Twist your body to the left, taking your weight on your right leg.

2 Turn your head to face the cast direction and untwist your body. Start to straighten your left arm. Your right hand should move in close to your chest.

3 Transfer your body we to your left leg. This increases the casting spee and makes for a really lon cast. Move your right han up towards eye level.

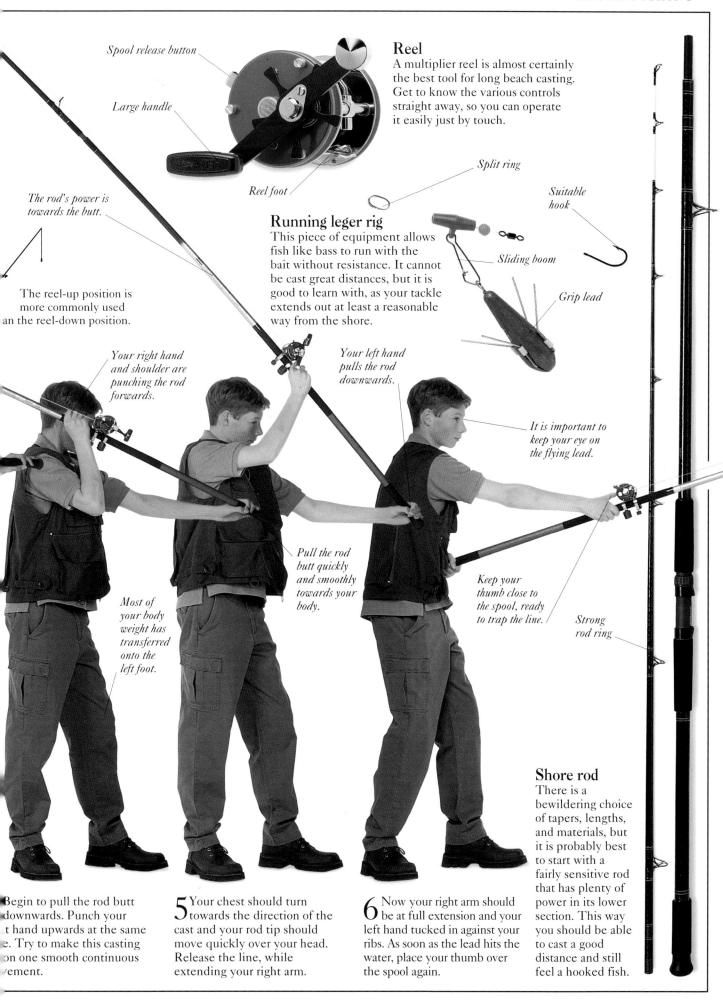

Spool release button

Reel
A multiplier reel is almost certainly the best tool for long beach casting. Get to know the various controls straight away, so you can operate it easily just by touch.

Large handle

Reel foot

Split ring

Suitable hook

Running leger rig
This piece of equipment allows fish like bass to run with the bait without resistance. It cannot be cast great distances, but it is good to learn with, as your tackle extends out at least a reasonable way from the shore.

Sliding boom

Grip lead

The rod's power is towards the butt.

The reel-up position is more commonly used an the reel-down position.

Your right hand and shoulder are punching the rod forwards.

Your left hand pulls the rod downwards.

It is important to keep your eye on the flying lead.

Pull the rod butt quickly and smoothly towards your body.

Most of your body weight has transferred onto the left foot.

Keep your thumb close to the spool, ready to trap the line.

Strong rod ring

egin to pull the rod butt downwards. Punch your
t hand upwards at the same
e. Try to make this casting
on one smooth continuous
vement.

5 Your chest should turn towards the direction of the cast and your rod tip should move quickly over your head. Release the line, while extending your right arm.

6 Now your right arm should be at full extension and your left hand tucked in against your ribs. As soon as the lead hits the water, place your thumb over the spool again.

Shore rod
There is a bewildering choice of tapers, lengths, and materials, but it is probably best to start with a fairly sensitive rod that has plenty of power in its lower section. This way you should be able to cast a good distance and still feel a hooked fish.

Reading the shoreline

AT FIRST SIGHT, the shore seems very long and the sea seems very large! Where do you begin looking for a particular species of sea fish? All sea fish have their own characteristic likes and dislikes and this makes the task of pinpointing them much easier. It is important to bear in mind seasons, depths, strength of the currents, the nature of the seabed and the availability of cover when you are deciding where to fish and for what.

The mullet is often called "the grey ghost" because of its ability to slide by unnoticed.

Mackerel

There are many types of mackerel, but all of the are long, streamlined, and have a markedly forke tail. Mackerel tend to move close inshore during summer months and can be found in huge shoals is best to drift in a boat when looking for them. feathers on a hook or small spinners as bait.

Grey mullet

Mullet tend to move northwards in the summer as the waters warm up. They feed on small organisms, but will eat larger food items when they are available. You will often find mullet around harbours, which they visit during high water. There they will scavenge for all types of titbits thrown in by passers-by. Try fishing for them with light float tackle and a piece of bread on a small hook.

Conger eel

These big eels tend to feed by night and rest by day close to piers, breakwaters, or anywhere they can find rocks or fallen debris to give them some shelter. They can also be found close to harbours, where they feed on unwanted scraps thrown away by fishermen. To catch them you will need a wire trace, a strong rod, and hefty line. Use large fish baits anchored on the sea bottom.

All members of the wrasse family have short, stumpy bodies.

Twine spot wrasse

Wrasse are lovers of rocks an cliffs, and this is where you shou try to find them. Wrasse have very strong lips and teeth, which they use to crush shellfish, abundant in these types of pla You can sometimes catch wrasse using a float, but more often by putting bait on the sea bottom. For use worms, crabs, and shellfish. Check the tides so you are never cut off by rising water.

The bass has a big mouth that can open wide to eat small fish.

You will never forget the fight from a decent-sized sea trout hooked in a running surf!

a bass

bass move close inshore during the summer months, and you will often
d them foraging up river mouths and feeding in brackish water. Look for
m around rocks and off piers – you may also find them where the surf
aks over sand. You can catch bass using worms and crabs, but possibly the
st exciting way to pursue them is with plugs and spinners. This method
ps you mobile, searching new areas until you find fish.

Sea trout

Sea trout are generally caught in rivers, but they can
also be taken from the shore. Look for sea trout around
rocks and river mouths or where there is a good surf
running. Sea trout are great foragers, and you can catch
them on worms, crabs, or small fish baits. The most fun
of all, however, is to spin for sea trout with silver-
coloured spoons or plugs about
10–12 cm (4–5 in) in length.

*Most flatfish lie along
sandy seabeds, feeding on
worms, small crabs, and
a variety of other
marine foodstuffs.*

atfish

tfish range from the smaller flounder,
ice, and sole, right up to the huge
ibut. They tend to be most active at
ht, but you can catch them during the
y if you fish the bait on the sea bottom.
y strips of dead fish or squid, or a bunch
worms. Flatfish sometimes attack small
nners cast a long way out from the shore.

Playing and landing your fish

PLAYING A FISH of any real size calls for patience, a cool head, and a lot of thought. Do not panic when you have finally got that long-awaited fish on the end of your line. Practise the skills shown here, get to know your reel controls and how to maximise the power of your rod, and with any luck, that fish will be yours.

Playing the fish

It is a good idea to practise at home on dry land, with a friend being the fish and pulling the line for you. This will teach you the limits of your tackle so that you know when you have to give line and when you can wind it in. This can save disappointment later on the riverbank.

Make sure your footing is secure and your body is perfectly balanced.

Notice how this rod ben throughout its length to take the strain of a plunging fish.

1 It is important to be comfortable when you are playing a fish, because some fights can be very long. Tuck the butt of the rod under your arm to give you better control and more power when lifting the rod.

The clutch
The clutch mechanism, located on the back of the reel, allows the spool to rotate under pressure so that line is given to a running fish. Adjust the clutch until you have exactly the right tension.

When you are playing a big fish, you will find that the power of the rod is in the lower sections.

Always hold the handle of the rod firmly but comfortably.

Get used to the feel of fly line. Be careful not to hold it too tightly, or the nylon leader will break.

Using fly tackle

Playing a fish on fly tackle is particularly thrilling. The fly rod is usually very light, so you can feel every plunge that the fish makes. When a hooked fish jumps, remember to lower your rod tip a fraction to give the line a little slack.

1 You may not need to use the reel very much when you are playing a fish on fly tackle. Instead, use your hands, letting line out when the fish runs and then retrieving the line when you sense the fish is tiring.

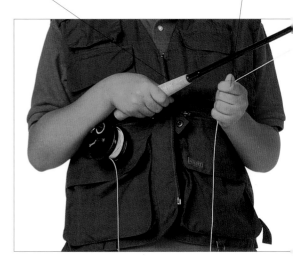

Keep the rod up
It is important to remember to keep the rod as high as possible to cushion all the plunges of the fish.

2 When the fish takes the fly and sets off in haste, feed line out to it through your fingers. When all the loose line around your feet is taken up by the running fish, it v begin to strip line off your reel in the normal fashion. Yo will soon sense how much pressure to exert on the fly lir so that it feeds smoothly to the fish without breaking.

*Keep the rod up high
as the fish comes in
to the bank.*

2 The critical moment is
when the fish is getting
close. Do not hurry it to the
net. Watch carefully and
once the fish is motionless
and on its side, draw it over
the submerged landing net.
Then lift the net and the
fish will fall into the meshes.

*Hold the handle of the net
firmly and with control.*

*Always choose a net
that is large enough
to engulf the catch.*

Catching and landing the fish

On the riverbank, it is often tempting to forget all you have learned in your
excitement and simply try to heave the fish over your shoulder and onto
dry land. Avoid this at all costs! Instead, remember the rules, keep a steady
pressure on the fish and, if your tackle is secure, you should be successful.
Check your line and knots before casting, because if there is any weakness
the fish will expose it. Also, make sure your landing net is close at hand. You
do not want to waste time looking for it when a fish is tired and ready to land.

1 Once the float has
gone under, you
are ready to strike.
Put in just the right
amount of pressure
to set the hook, but
not so much that the
line breaks. You will
have to strike quite
hard for long
distances, but for
striking close by, a
simple flick of the
wrist will do.

2 Once again, keep
the rod high. You
will find that this
gives a cushioning
effect, absorbing
any dashes the fish
might make and
protecting the line
as well.

*Notice that the landing
net is close at hand,
ready for action.*

*Set the clutch on your fly reel so
that it gives line to a running
fish under pressure.*

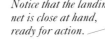

3 Once the fish surfaces and you can
pull its head clear out of the water,
you will know it is beaten and
ready for the net. Do not try to net
a fish if it is still very lively. If the
fish is heavy, be prepared to lift
the net by the frame rather than
the handle.

*A beaten fish, too tired
to struggle any further.*

*Pull the line
back in a slow,
controlled way.*

4 Keep the net fairly
still in the water
and draw the fish
over it. Once you are
quite sure that all of
the fish is over the
rim, lift the net gently
and steadily out of
the water and onto the
bank. Do not pursue
the fish with the net,
or you run the risk
of knocking it off
the hook.

When the fish at last grows tired, start manoeuvring
it back towards the bank. Trap the line against the
handle with the fingers of one hand. With your free
nd slowly pull the line back in, avoiding any jerky
ovements. Try to anticipate the fish's movements and
prepared to give it line if it wants to run out again.

Releasing your catch

WELL DONE! You have caught your fish and it is lying there in the net. However, remember that you have a great responsibility to treat that fish as carefully and considerately as you can, and to return it to the water unharmed. In the water, fish may look strong and powerful, but bear in mind that the effect on them of being lifted out of their natural environment can be very traumatic.

Safety near water
Take extra care when standing on slippery banks.

A prize catch

I was very proud of this catch and wanted a photograph. However, it was a hot day and I knew that this would cause the fish some distress, so the shot had to be taken very quickly. I had already focused the camera before I took the fish from the water, and I made sure I held it over the water's edge in case it wriggled free.

Notice the way I am holding this fish, with my hands away from any vital organs.

Unhooking and releasing

Always treat any fish you catch as gently as you possibly can, whatever its size. Make sure you wet your hands before you handle the fish, or you may disturb the coat of slime or mucus that surrounds the fish and protects it from disease.

As you become used to handling fish, you will know just how much pressure to exert.

1 Once you have lifted your fish out of the water, it is important that you hold it firmly to prevent it from wriggling free and falling to the ground. Remember not to squeeze it too hard though, or you could damage its vital organs.

2 If you are right-handed, hold the fish in your left han and take the hook out with your stronger fingers. If the hook is barbless, it should slip free very easily. Shou there be a problem, simply wriggle the hook gently wit your fingers and it will soon drop away.

38

Under pressure
Always keep cool when you are handling a fish and try not to panic – even when it starts to wriggle!

This is a critical moment. You have to return the fish to the water, but you must also be aware of your own safety. If the [ban]k is high, look for a safe entry point nearby. When you place [the] fish in the water, make sure you crouch down on the bank in [a co]mfortable, stable position. If possible, have a friend there in [case] you fall. Never take chances.

Watch your fish very carefully after you have slipped it into the water. Do not release it until it is strong enough to hold its own [aga]inst the current. Never let a fish go off down river belly-up, [be]cause it will be unable to right itself and will certainly die. If you [do], let the fish lie in the soft weeds along the bank until it recovers.

Releasing underwater

If you are fishing a shallow stretch of river where you can wade safely, it is often possible to release a fish completely underwater. This reduces any stress the fish may suffer. Unless a fish is particularly unusual, you do not really need to look at it carefully. The bite and the fight should be exciting enough and then you can wish it a fond farewell! Never use a keep-net, unless you are fishing in a match, as these cause the fish untold physical and mental harm.

1 This chub is now exhausted and ready for landing, but it is not really necessary to remove it from the water to be admired and then released. Bringing it onto the bank will cause a certain amount of stress, which can be avoided by unhooking it entirely underwater.

The fish is on its side and is tired enough for the hook to be removed.

2 With a fairly small fish like this one, there is no need even to use a landing net. Lower your rod to take the tension off the line and slip the hook out with your fingers. Providing it is barbless, it will come free at once. Get ready to support the fish with your free hand.

3 The fish is now ready for release, even though it has not yet broken the surface. To give it some time to recover its strength before it swims away into the powerful current, hold it facing upstream until you feel its fins begin to pulse and its muscles flex. There is now no danger of it rolling over and being unable to right itself, so you can let it go.

Fish directory

THERE ARE NEARLY twenty thousand types of fish swimming in the world's freshwaters and seas and it is exciting to get to know as much as possible about the many different species and their various characteristics. Even though it would be impossible to catch them all, it is good to look for as many different types as you can, rather than specializing in one species. In doing so, you will learn much about the amazing world that exists beneath the water's surface.

The pike's fins are heavily camouflaged.

The dark spot on the dorsal fin is a hallmark of the bluegill.

Bluegill

The bluegill is the most popular panfish in N America and it is distributed throughou most of the states. It is a good fighte although it rarely grows very large and it can be caught on flies, sr spinners, and different types bait. Look for it sheltering amongst weed or tree roc

Large fins give the bluegill plenty of power.

The fully formed tail fin suggests a fish born in the wild.

The huge tail fin gives the carp its power.

The long, muscular body of the sturgeon makes it a great fighter.

Carp

The carp is the most popular freshwater fish in Europe It grows to at least 27 kg (60 lb), fights very hard, and is difficult to outwit. You can catch carp either on the bottom or using baits floating on the surface.

Sturgeon

There are around twenty types of sturgeon swimming the waters of the world and many of them can be caught by anglers. These fish can easily grow to 140 kg (300 lb) or more and are generally caught using a large fish bait close to the bottom. Sea tackle will usually be needed to land fish like this.

The sturgeon uses its pointed nose for digging up prey from the silt.

The positioning of the eyes allows the pike to see prey fish swimming overhead.

The mottled flanks of the pike allow it to merge in with its surroundings.

Big pectorals give the pike swift acceleration.

Pike

Pike are the supreme freshwater predators of the northern hemisphere and popular with competition anglers. A 9 kg (20 lb) pike is a good size, but they can grow to 18 kg (40 lb) or more. Pike are at home in both rivers and stillwaters and are usually found lurking amongst reeds, sunken logs, and boulders.

Salmon

There cannot be a more dramatic and amazing fish than the salmon. Watch them leap waterfalls and overcome all obstacles in their journey from the sea back into freshwater to spawn and die.

Chub have big, brassy scales and a thick, heavy body.

Chub

The chub is a medium-sized European freshwater fish beloved by anglers, because it will take almost any type of bait in any water conditions.

The trout's large mouth allows it to eat fish as well as insects.

Brown trout

The brown trout varies greatly in size and appearance. There are over fifty types of this species in Europe alone. It is a very popular gaming fish, because it has a suspicious nature and is very hard to catch.

The spiny dorsal fin is partly joined to the soft-rayed second dorsal.

Large-mouth bass

The large-mouth bass is arguably the favourite sport fish in North America. It has been widely distributed around the world because of its power, cunning, and willingness to attack lures, flies, and baits.

The bass has a deep, mottled-green body and a pronounced lateral line.

The eye of the zander is opaque, giving it a glassy look.

Zander

The European zander is very much like its North American cousin, the walleye. Both species grow to 7–9 kg (15–20 lb) and feed especially well at dusk, through the night, and at dawn. Try using small, dead fish or medium-sized spoons and plugs to catch them.

Taking it further

O NE OF THE WONDERFUL things about fishing is that it can lead you to exotic, faraway places. As your experience increases, your confidence will grow and you will want to take on new challenges, catch new types of fish, and learn new skills. No matter how many years you spend angling, there will always be more exciting new waters to discover.

Wild river fishing

The really big, gushing rivers of the world present a huge challenge to both fly and lure anglers alike. You have to learn to control your tackle in the swiftest of waters, where huge fish often lurk. It is hair-raising, white-knuckle stuff that demands both your technique and tackle to be flawless!

Fly tying

On long, dark winter evenings, you may want to try tying your own flies. Making perfect imitations of the natural flies on which fish feed is an exact, truly satisfying science. You may find that your own flies are more successful than expensive, shop-bought ones.

The mighty mahseer

This angler looks delighted with his catch – and no wonder! This enormous mahseer was caught in a huge river in southern India and fought for over an hour and a half in fast-flowing water. It weighed over 40 kg (90 lb) and was a record for that stretch of water. Truly the catch of a lifetime!

Over 100 years ago, British officers in India used the mahseer's huge scales as playing cards.

Boat fishing

As you become more experienced, you may want to move away from the bank and try the different skills involved in boat fishing. Boat control is a whole new art in itself and requires much practice. Landing a large fish from a boat can be very tricky, as it demands perfect timing.

Never do anything quickly when you are in a boat. Every movement should be calm and controlled. It is advisable to wear a life-jacket.

hing the wilderness

e I am fishing for colossal catfish on a
lerness river in the Himalayas of Nepal.
ok three days to reach this remote water
re, I was told, no other European had
ed before. This was the perfect location:
p water, a gliding current, and numerous
s for huge prey fish to hide behind.

The tropical seas

You may be lucky enough to travel to exotic places such as Christmas Tree Island, above, and fish the warm oceans that surround it. The shallows in tropical seas tend to be richer in fish than those in cooler waters. Countless varieties of fish roam the shallows (called the Flats) of this crystal-clear water. This snapper has come in close to the shore to feed off the colourful coral reefs.

Night fishing

Nothing can beat the serenity of night fishing for utter peace. It is often a good idea to fish at night if waters are so clear that anglers are visible to the fish in the daytime.

Considerate angling

REMEMBER THAT WHENEVER you are by the waterside you are on show, a representative of our sport. Always read the rules that the club or owner has laid down for the water; they are for everybody's good, yours included, and you should follow them to the letter. Avoid putting any life at risk, whether it be yours, another angler's, or that of a fish, a bird, livestock, or a wild animal. Enjoy the beauty of the river, but always remember to be considerate!

Canoeists

Remember that we are not the only people with a right to use the water. Swimmers, walkers, sailors, water-skiers, an even scuba divers all enjoy water sports. Canoeists can se a problem on some rivers, but they will nearly always mov across river and out of your way. Be reassured that most fi are not disturbed by the presence of canoes.

Kingfisher

Sit quietly on the riverbank and you will hear the thin piping call of the kingfisher as it speeds past in a blur of blue. If you are lucky, this fellow angler may actually land on your rod tip. It is a rare and magical moment that should be treasured.

Dusk and dawn are the best times to see an otter.

Otter

Otters are quite large and very sh so do not confuse them with th bolder, smaller mink that frequent so many riverbank The otter is a sure sign tha the water you are fishing i well stocked, so it is a welcome sighting indeed. If you do see an otter, congratulate yourself; it is proof that you are a quiet, considerate angler who respec the countryside and its wildlife.

Closing gates

Always shut gates behind you, otherwise livestock could escape onto roads, causing fatal accidents. Be sure that you shut a gate properly. Check that you have fastened it exactly as you found it, as it could work loose in a strong wind or if cattle push against it.

Countryside awareness

Always stick to well-defined pathways, especially if you are walking to the waterside through crops. Use a stile wherever possible, rather than climbing over and perhaps damaging a fence. If you are fishing with a dog and there are sheep about, keep your dog on a lead. Never light a fire in windy, dry conditions.

Climb stiles carefully if they are greasy after rain.

Picking up your line

Never leave discarded line on the bank, for it can easily become entangled in the legs of animals and birds. Unable to fly or run off, they are doomed to a lingering death. Take special care never to leave a baited hook on any piece of nylon, in case a bird decides to eat it and dies as a result.

Discarded nylon will take years to rot.

Noise

Noise travels very freely over water. You can be heard by other anglers who may seem a long way off. Please do not shout or run about and, most importantly, do not have a radio blaring. Nearly all anglers go fishing to escape the hustle and bustle of modern-day life, not to be reminded of it.

Show consideration for all enclosed animals.

Take notice of the signs

Waterside signs are put there for your good or the good of the water. If you are asked to take only four fish, that is because any more would ruin the chances of other anglers. Watch out especially for any danger signs. They might warn about deep water, slippery banks, or overhead power lines.

Always read signs.

Glossary

You will find many of these words useful during your days on the river.

A

Adipose fin The small, fleshy fin on the back of fish from the salmon family.
Avon float A float used for fishing in fast water. The top of the float is fairly buoyant, which allows it to ride the current well.

B

Backing Fine, strong braid or nylon of 100 m (320 ft) or more, put on a fly reel, underneath the standard fly line. Essential for playing large fish.
Backwind Giving line to a running fish by simply letting go of the handle and letting the reel move in reverse. Not used very often today, as clutches are more efficient.
Bag limit The limit trout fisheries put on the amount of fish that can be caught.
Bale arm The metal arm on a fixed-spool reel. It helps to guide the line onto the spool.
Barb A sharp piece of metal on the hook.
Barbles Whiskery fingers of flesh that hang down from the sides of many fish's mouths.
Bite A term for when a fish has taken the bait.
Bivvies A common name for bivouacs.
Boilies Boiled baits, usually made out of eggs, flavourings, colourings, soya, and other additives, boiled and rolled into small balls for easy casting.
Braid lines A thinner alternative to nylon lines.
Breaking strain The weight limit that lines can carry before they break, e.g., 1 kg (2.2 lb).
Butt The rod handle.

C

Carbon fibre Very light and strong material, used in most fishing rods.
Casters The chrysalis form of maggots. The bluebottle develops within the shell and emerges when ready to fly.
Clutch A mechanism in the reel that allows line to be taken off under different pressures.
Coarse fish A British term to

describe freshwater fish that do not belong to the salmon family.
Cocked The position of a float when it is sitting vertically in the water.

D

Dorsal fin The fin at the top of a fish's back. These take many forms; in the perch and bass family they are spiked.
Down-rigger A mechanism that takes spinning baits down into the deep areas of large lakes.
Dry-fly fishing Fishing a floating fly on the surface of the water.

E

Eddy A piece of slow and often deep water, just off the main current of a river.

F

False casting Moving a rod backwards and forwards a few times before casting. Fly fishermen do this to work more line out before letting it lie on the surface of the water.
Floating line Used when fishing a dry fly or a small nymph just under the surface.
Forceps Scissor-like tool used to remove hooks from fish's mouths.
Foul-hooked Any fish that is not hooked on the mouth.
Fry Tiny fish that have just emerged from eggs after spawning time.

G

Game fish Fish belonging to the salmon family (including trout and grayling).
Groundbait Any bait thrown into a fishing area to stimulate fish to feed.

H

Hatch A group of newly hatched flies that stimulate trout and grayling into feeding.

I

Ice fishing Fishing through ice.

J

Jerk baits Very big plugs which are fished w stiff, short rods. They are pulled or jerked though the water erratically.
Jigging Fishing from boats with baits direct beneath the rods, moving the rod up and dow to give it life. Often a small spinner or a little plastic worm is used as bait.

L

Landing net A net used to scoop a beaten fi out of the water and to lay it onto the bank.
Leader A stretch of nylon that is attached to the end of a fly line. The imitation fly is tied the point of the leader.
Leads Lead weights used to sink a bait. Lea weighing 14–110 g ($^1/_2$–4 oz) are used in freshwater legering. In sea fishing the leads c be much heavier.
Legering The style of fishing which puts a l right on the bottom, often anchored by a hea load.
Lie A place where a fish, generally a trout, li to live. A trout will have its own lie for most o its life.
Live bait Any bait that is live, such as fish, frogs, or grasshoppers.
Loose feed Samples of the hook bait scatter around a fishing area to encourage fish to fee
Lures A general name given to spinners, spoons, and plugs – all imitations of small fish

M

Maggots The small, white grubs of bluebott A very popular bait for small freshwater fish.
Mending the line Correcting a line that has been pushed into a bow shape by a river's current. It is done by lifting the rod tip, allow the float to travel downstream in a natural wa
Mucus The protective slimy coating on mos fish that prevents disease.

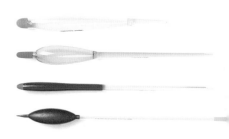

nph fishing Using small flies that imitate
phs in water to catch trout and grayling.

fish Small American freshwater fish, such
uegill or sunfish.

stic worms Imitation worms that are
ched onto a weighted hook and usually
ed for small predators like perch zander.

ying a fish Line, reel, and rod control when
ding in a bite.

aroid glasses Glasses with special lenses
filter out the reflections on the water's
ace. They make it possible to see what the
are doing under the water.

es Very long, light fishing rods – often up to
m (50 ft) in length. These are used in match
ing to catch lots of small fish quickly.

ol A slow, deep area of water found along a
r, often behind rocks or fallen trees.

y fish Fish that are the diet of predators.

ivertip A thin piece of material spliced into
top of a rod to indicate delicate bites.

l seat A device that attaches a reel to a rod.
le A fast, shallow, broken area of river where
will find trout and grayling.

gs The rings on a rod which guide the line.

e The action of a fish coming to the surface
sipping in a floating insect.

rest A metal stick with a V-shaped top
igned to cradle the rod when it is not being
d. Very useful for legering.

n When a fish darts away from the angler
e it has been hooked.

les Hard pieces of
y tissue that
ect a fish's body.
e age of a fish can
ead from the growth
g on an individual scale.

sons Nearly all fish have seasons when they
be caught and when they must be left alone.
h are generally considered out of season
ing their spawning period.

ot Weights that are used to present the bait
ifferent depths.

king line A line used by fly anglers when
y want their flies to reach trout and salmon
r the bottom of a river or lake.

ag An underwater obstruction.

nar An electronic device attached to a boat,
ich gives a reading of how deep the water is.
netimes it will show up shoals of fish or large
ividual fish.

ool The part of the reel that holds the line.

lking A method of angling by observing the
in the water. It requires great care and skill.

ike The act of quickly pulling up a rod to set
hook into a biting fish.

im The area of water being fished,
ecially by bait anglers.

im feeders Cylinders of plastic or metal,
ched to a line close to the hook, that take
ples of bait down to the bed of a river or lake.

T

Take A fish biting upon a fly (especially grayling or trout).

Telescopic rods Rods that can slide down into short, compact lengths.

Terminal tackle All the tackle attached to the end of the main line, such as hooks, floats, weights, and lures.

Test curve The strength of a rod defined by the weight needed to bend it. A typical freshwater rod has a test curve of 0.5 kg (1 lb).

Treble hook A hook with three points, usually found on all types of lures.

Trolling A method by which natural or artificial bait is pulled long distances through water behind a boat. The bait can be fished at almost any depth and is intended to resemble a live fish.

W

Wading Walking out into a river to fish an area more effectively or to get closer to the fish.

Wet fly A fly that is fished underneath the surface for trout and grayling.

Whippings The rod rings are attached to the rod by whippings, generally made of silk.

Anglers' Conservation Association

Useful addresses

Jane James (Director)
Shalford Dairy
Aldermaston
Reading
Berks RG7 4NB
(The group works tirelessly against pollution. Join as a junior member and receive a badge, magazines, etc.)
(0118) 971 4770
admin@a-c-a.org

British Waterways
Brindley Suite, Willow Grange
Church Road
Watford
Herts WD1 3QA
(All you need to know about fishing canals around Britain.)
(01442) 235400

Game Angling Instructors Association
Mike Levins
Little Saxbys Farm
Cowden
Edenbridge
Kent TN8 7DX
(Write for a list of instructors in you area.)
(01342) 850765

Game Fishing Association of Australia
Secretary
PO Box A168
Shellharbour, New South Wales
NSW 2529, Australia
(02) 4296 5434
www.gfaa.asn.au

New Zealand Federation of Fresh Water Anglers (NZFFA)
Secretary
499 Albert Street
Palmerston North
New Zealand
(06) 356 5537

Index

Acknowledgments

Dorling Kindersley would like to thank the following people for their help in the production of this book:

Special thanks to all the young anglers for their enthusiasm and patience during the photo shoots, and also their families; Ken Aske for assisting in our search for young anglers; Mike Taylor and Wendy Vane-Percy for food and accommodation; Gary Barclay and Drennan International, Harris Angling, Sportfish, and Farlow's, for supplying angling equipment; John Partridge Limited for their involvement in the project and advice; Andy Komorowski for photographic assistance; Joanna Buck, Lee Simmons, and Selina Wood for

editorial assistance; and Giles Powell-Smith for the jacket design.

Picture credits
The publisher would like to thank the following for their kind permission to reproduce their photographs:
a = above; *c* = centre; *b* = below/bottom; *l* = left; *r* = right; *t* = top.
Ancient Art & Architecture Collection: 5*clb*; **John Bailey:** 4*crb*, *cra*, *cl*, *tl*; 5*b*; 38*tr*; 42*cr*, *b*, 42–43*tc*, 43*bcl*; 44*bl*, *c*, 44–45*tc*; **Andrew Beasley Photolibrary:** 34–35*c*;

Biofotos: 34*bl*; **Richard T. Bryant:** 9*cl*, 40*c*, 40–41*b*; **Kevin Cullimore:** 20*c*, 21*tr*, 26*tr*; **Mary Evans Picture Library:** 5*cr*; **E.T. Archive:** 5*tl*; **Robert Harding Picture Library:** Michel le Coz 32*tr*; **Johnny Jensen:** 42*b*; **JPH Foto:** 9*crb*, 24*cl*, *br*, 25*br*, *tl*, 27*tr*, 35*tr*; **NHPA: Agence Nature** 42*cl*; **OSF:** Richard Davies jacket, p6–7; **Oxford Scientific Films:** E.R. Derringer 9*cra*; Andreas Hartl Okapia 9*tr*; Colin Milkins 9*br*; Peter Parks 7*ca*; **Planet Earth Pictures:** Paulo de Oliveira 35*tl*; Linda Pitkin 34*tr*; John F. Seagrim 34*cl*; James D. Watt 43*tr*.